WEEKLY **WR** READER®
EARLY LEARNING LIBRARY

HOW SIMPLE MACHINES WORK

HOW LEVERS WORK

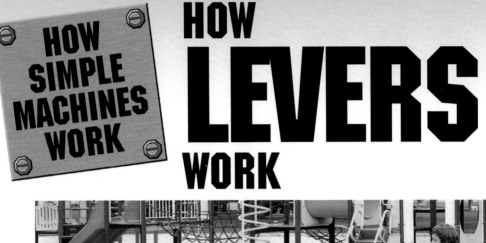

by **Jim Mezzanotte**

Reading consultant: Susan Nations, M.Ed.,
author/literacy coach/consultant

Science and curriculum consultant: Debra Voege, M.A.,
science and math curriculum resource teacher

Please visit our web site at: www.garethstevens.com
For a free color catalog describing Weekly Reader® Early Learning Library's list
of high-quality books, call 1-877-445-5824 (USA) or 1-800-387-3178 (Canada).
Weekly Reader® Early Learning Library's fax: (414) 336-0164.

Library of Congress Cataloging-in-Publication Data

Mezzanotte, Jim.
    How levers work / by Jim Mezzanotte.
       p. cm. — (How simple machines work)
    Includes bibliographical references and index.
    ISBN-10: 0-8368-7347-5 — ISBN-13: 978-0-8368-7347-4 (lib. bdg.)
    ISBN-10: 0-8368-7352-1 — ISBN-13: 978-0-8368-7352-8 (softcover)
    1. Levers—Juvenile literature. I. Title.
  II. Series: Mezzanotte, Jim. How simple machines work.
  TJ147.M49   2006
  621.8—dc22   2006008668

This edition first published in 2007 by
Weekly Reader® Early Learning Library
A Member of the WRC Media Family of Companies
330 West Olive Street, Suite 100
Milwaukee, WI 53212 USA

Copyright © 2007 by Weekly Reader® Early Learning Library

Managing editor: Mark J. Sachner
Art direction: Tammy West
Cover design, page layout, and illustrations: Dave Kowalski
Photo research: Sabrina Crewe

Picture credits: cover, title, p. 11 © Michelle D. Bridwell/Photo Edit; p. 5 © Christina
Kennedy/Photo Edit; p. 6 © Ariel Skelley/CORBIS; p. 12 © Royalty-Free/CORBIS; p. 16
© George Shelley/CORBIS; p. 18 © Mika/zefa/CORBIS; p. 19 © Paul Barton/CORBIS; p. 20
© Royalty-Free/CORBIS; p. 21 © Tony Freeman/Photo Edit

Printed in the United States of America

1 2 3 4 5 6 7 8 9 10 09 08 07 06

TABLE OF CONTENTS

Cover and title page: A seesaw is an example of a lever.

CHAPTER

THE WORLD OF LEVERS

Have you ever played on a seesaw? Hit a ball with
a bat? Flipped a light switch? If so, then you have
used a lever.

4

Levers are all around you. They make it easier for people to do things like lifting or moving something heavy. Levers help make many jobs easier.

When you turn on a light, you are using a lever.

The oars
of a boat
are levers.

Levers come in many different forms. A hammer can
be a lever. Scissors, pliers, and can openers are levers.
Wheelbarrows and brooms are also levers. So are the
oars in a rowboat. Even your body has levers. Your jaw is
a lever. Your arms are levers, too. Levers are everywhere!

CHAPTER 2

HOW LEVERS WORK

You can make your own lever. A lever should not bend much. Let's use a wooden ruler as a lever. A lever always **pivots**, or tilts, on something. The point where it pivots is called the **fulcrum**. Place a big crayon crosswise under the ruler. The load is what the lever moves against. Let's use a can for the load. It rests on one end of the ruler.

Your lever has two parts. One part is between the **load** and the fulcrum. It is called the **load arm**. The other part is between the fulcrum and your **effort**. It is called the **effort arm**. When you push down on the end of the effort arm, that is your effort. Your effort lifts the can.

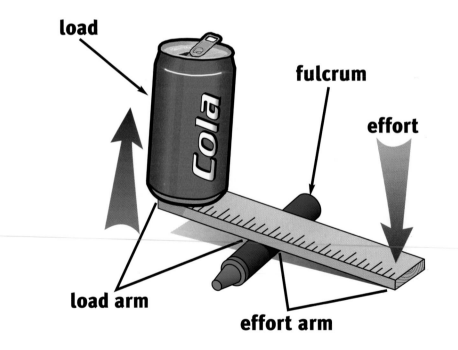

load

fulcrum

effort

load arm

effort arm

Try moving the fulcrum away from the load. The effort arm is shorter, so you must use more effort to lift the can.

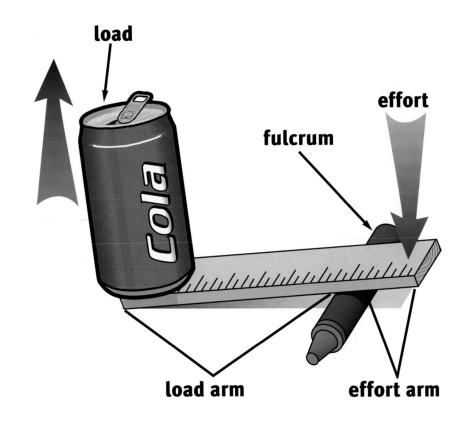

load

effort

fulcrum

load arm

effort arm

Next, move the fulcrum closer to the load. Now the effort arm is longer. So you push farther down to lift the can, but you use less effort.

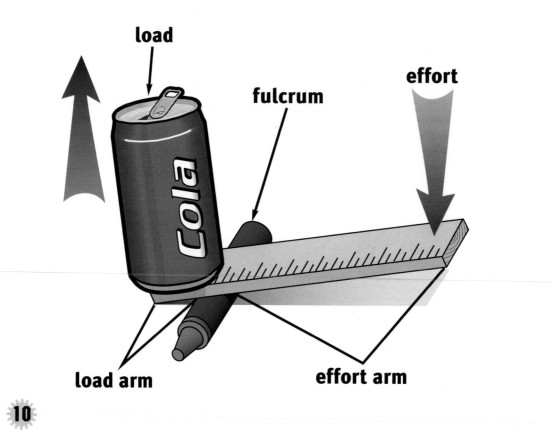

load

effort

fulcrum

load arm

effort arm

A seesaw is a special lever that we see on a playground. The fulcrum is the pivot point in the center. First one side of the seesaw is the load arm and the other side is the effort arm. Then the first side becomes the effort arm and the other becomes the load arm.

This seesaw is a lever. As each side of the seesaw is lowered and raised, the children take turns being the load and using effort.

CHAPTER

KINDS OF LEVERS

Your ruler and the playground seesaw are examples of a **first-class lever**. On each, the fulcrum is between the effort and the load. A can opener is also a first-class lever. So is a hammer when you use it to pull nails out of a board. Scissors and pliers are double first-class levers. Each handle is a lever. The fulcrum is where the handles cross.

A wheelbarrow is a **second-class lever**. Its fulcrum is the wheel at one end. The load is between the fulcrum and the effort.

load

fulcrum

effort

Wheelbarrows are second-class levers. They help people lift heavy loads.

Your jaw is a second-class lever. The fulcrum is where it attaches to your skull. The load is what you chew. A nutcracker is a double second-class lever. The two handles are levers. The fulcrum is the hinge at the end.

The two handles of a nutcracker are levers. Together they make a simple machine that cracks a hard nut.

fulcrum

Did you ever use a broom? It is a **third-class lever**. The fulcrum is where you hold it on top. The load is what you sweep. Your effort is in the middle, where you put the other hand.

effort

load

A broom is a lever. This boy is using it to clear away leaves quickly.

Your arms are third-class levers. Your elbows are fulcrums and your hands hold the load. The effort comes from your muscles.

A baseball bat is a lever. It lets you hit a ball far.

First-class and second-class levers let you move heavy loads with little effort. Third-class levers take more effort, but move loads a long distance. When you swing a baseball bat, it is a third-class lever. Hitting a home run takes effort, but the ball zooms far.

CHAPTER

JOBS FOR LEVERS

People have been using levers for thousands of years. Early hunters made levers out of sticks and rocks. People still use levers to pry rocks from the ground. Scissors, pliers, and wheelbarrows have been around for many years, too.

Long ago, a man named Archimedes learned how levers work. He knew that a long lever could lift very heavy things. He said he could lift the world if he had a long enough lever—and could find a fulcrum to rest it on.

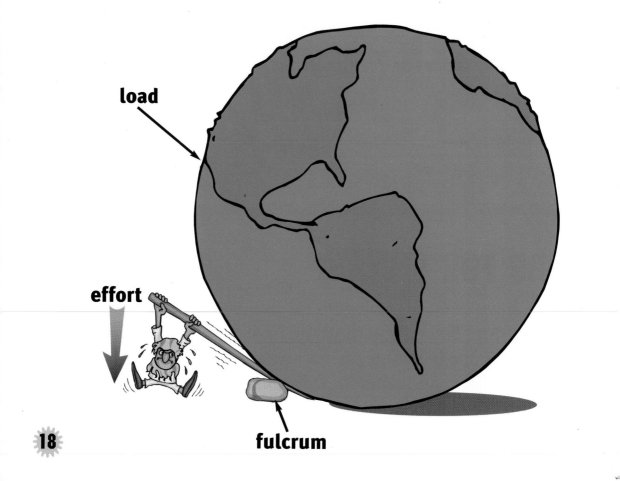

load

effort

fulcrum

The spokes on these bike wheels act as levers.

Did you know that a wheel is a **simple machine**? Picture the **spokes** of a wheel. The spokes act like levers. They pivot all the way around the **axle,** which is the fulcrum.

Long arms on this machine help it dig. The arms are levers.

Today, many machines use levers. Digging machines use buckets attached to big arms. The arms are levers.

Even a stapler is a lever. Wherever you find them, levers help people get the job done!

fulcrum

Do you ever use a stapler? It is a lever, too!

21

GLOSSARY

axle: the shaft at the center of a wheel. The axle acts like a fulcrum, around which the wheel's spokes pivot.

effort: the force, or action, that moves a lever

effort arm: the part of a lever between the effort and the fulcrum

first-class lever: a lever with the fulcrum between the effort and the load

fulcrum: the point on which a lever pivots. The fulcrum can be at the end or anywhere in the middle of a lever.

load: anything that a lever moves against. A load can be a pile of dirt in a wheelbarrow, a ball hit by a bat, or a nut crushed by a nutcracker.

load arm: the part of a lever between the load and the fulcrum

pivots: tilts, or turns, around a single point

second-class lever: a lever with the load between the fulcrum and the effort

simple machines: devices with few or no moving parts. They let you do a lot of work without a lot of effort.

spokes: strong bars that go from a wheel's outer rim to its inner hub. The spokes act like the levers pivoting around the axle.

third-class lever: a lever with the effort between the fulcrum and the load

FOR MORE INFORMATION

BOOKS

How Can I Experiment with a Lever? How Can I Experiment with
Simple Machines? *(series).* David Armentrout (Rourke Publishing)

Sensational Science Projects with Simple Machines. Fantastic Physical
Science Experiments (series). Robert Gardner (Enslow Publishers)

WEB SITES

Edheads: Simple Machines
edheads.org/activities/simple-machines/
At this interactive site, you can learn all about simple machines,
including pulleys.

Levers: Simple Machines
www.enchantedlearning.com/physics/machines/Levers.shtml
Visit this site to see diagrams and examples of different levers.

Mikids.com: Simple Machines
www.mikids.com/Smachines.htm
This site has examples of simple machines, including pulleys. It also
has fun activities to help you learn more about simple machines.

Publisher's note to educators and parents: Our editors have carefully reviewed these
Web sites to ensure that they are suitable for children. Many Web sites change frequently,
however, and we cannot guarantee that a site's future contents will continue to meet
our high standards of quality and educational value. Be advised that children should
be closely supervised whenever they access the Internet.

INDEX

About the Author

Jim Mezzanotte has written many books for children. He lives in Milwaukee with his wife and two sons. He uses simple machines every day.